THE FINGER OF GOD

Stories of Wisdom, Direction & Healing

Published by Hear My Heart Publishing

Copyright 2016 Beth Wilson

All rights reserved. No part of this book may be reproduced or transmitted in any form or by any electronic or mechanical means, including photocopying, recording, or by any information storage and retrieval system, without the written permission of the publisher, except where permitted by law.

ISBN: 978-0-9862331-5-9

A product of the United States of America.

Edited by Gene LaViness and Michelle Lehman

Table of Contents

Preface   1

God Works in Mysterious Ways   4
Beth S. Wilson

His Way is the Best Way   6
Darlene Shortridge

God Knows My Heart   12
Karen Forsythe

Open all Your Gifts   17
Lisa Bain

Ten Years of Jehovah-Jireh   19
John and Deborah Butler

We Gave it our Best Shot   25
Bridget Johnson

Hearing God's Voice	27
Bridget Johnson	
Story two	
Yes Lord	28
Judi E. Grove	
Once a Missionary Always a Missionary	29
Judi Grove	
Story two	
Miracles	31
Debbie Noble	
Lessons Learned	36
Harold Bloom	
Healing from Above	41
Judy Bloom	
Too Close for Comfort	43
Beth S. Wilson	

Tears From the Heart	44
Penney Camper	
Make the Connection	47
Penney Camper	
Story Two	
God is Good	50
Susan Miller	
Gifts From God	51
M.N. Morrow	
Perfect Peace	53
Kerrie Tims	
How God Has Worked in My Life	54
Mark Berrier	
God's Timing	56
Jerri Ann Currey	

I Am Healed	57
Bethany Duarte	
Inside a Russian Orphanage	64
Stephanie Reno	
Empowered to Win	66
Naomi Damron	
That Still Small Voice	68
Doc Woods	
The Gift	70
Rosie Maureen	
Eighteen Days After Her Death	74
Michelle Lehman	

This book is dedicated to bringing honor and glory to God.

Preface

How many times has something happened and you have known without a shadow of a doubt that it was God directed?

This book is an opportunity to tell some of those stories and to give Praise and Honor to God for his provision.

I am reminded of a story I read in 1 Kings.

King Ahab reigned in Samaria over Israel for twenty-two years. He did evil in the sight of God, more than all who came before him. The King wanted the vineyard that was beside his palace and the owner would not sell it to him. The King's wife, Jezebel, had the vineyard owner killed and told her husband to take possession of the property and he did.

The Lord sent the prophet Elijah with a word for the King. Starting in 1 Kings 21, verse 19:

"Say to him, 'This is what the LORD says: Have you not murdered a man and seized his property?' Then say to him, 'This is what the LORD says: In the place where dogs licked up Naboth's blood, **dogs will lick up your blood**—yes, yours!'"(emphasis mine)

Ahab said to Elijah, "So you have found me, my enemy!"

"I have found you," he answered, "because you have sold yourself to do evil in the eyes of the LORD. He says, 'I am going to bring disaster on you. I will wipe out your descendants and cut off from Ahab every last male in Israel—slave or free. I will make your house like that of Jeroboam son of Nebat and that of Baasha son of Ahijah, because you have aroused my anger and have caused Israel to sin.'

"And also concerning Jezebel the LORD says: 'Dogs will devour Jezebel by the wall of Jezreel.'

"Dogs will eat those belonging to Ahab who die in the city, and the birds will feed on those who die in the country."

When Ahab heard these words, he tore his clothes, put on sackcloth and fasted. He lay in sackcloth and went around meekly.

Then the word of the LORD came to Elijah: "Have you noticed how Ahab has humbled himself before me? Because he has humbled himself, I will not bring this disaster in his day, but I will bring it on his house in the days of his son."

Three years later:

1 Kings 22 starting in verse 29:

"So the king of Israel and Jehoshaphat king of Judah went up to Ramoth Gilead. **The king of Israel said** to Jehoshaphat, "**I will enter the battle in disguise**, but you wear your royal robes." So the king of Israel disguised himself and went into battle.

Now the king of Aram had ordered his thirty-two chariot commanders, "Do not fight with anyone, small or great, except the king of Israel." When the chariot commanders saw Jehoshaphat, they thought, "Surely this is the king of Israel." So they turned to attack him, but when Jehoshaphat cried out, the chariot commanders saw that he was not the king of Israel and stopped pursuing him.

But **someone drew his bow at random and hit the king of Israel between the sections of his armor**. The king told his chariot driver, "Wheel around and get me out of the fighting. I've been wounded." All day long the battle raged, and the king was propped up in his chariot facing the Arameans. The blood from his wound ran onto the floor of the chariot, and that evening he died. As the sun was setting, a cry spread through the army: "Every man to his town. Every man to his land!"

So the king died and was brought to Samaria, and they buried him there. They washed the chariot at a pool in Samaria (where the prostitutes bathed), **and the dogs licked up his blood, as the word of the LORD had declared**."

Did you see what happened? I highlighted a couple of sections; I don't want you to miss this. A random arrow, shot into the air found its way into a section of the King's armor and fulfilled God's word. My husband preached a sermon called The

Finger of God. God directed that stray arrow exactly where He wanted it to go and that arrow did exactly what God wanted. It was not by chance. It was directed by the finger of God.

Again, how many times has something happened and you have known without a shadow of a doubt that it was God directed?

The people's stories you are about to read are exactly that. They are not professional authors. They are ordinary people who want to give God the glory for what He has done in their life.

May God be honored with the publication of this book.

God Works in Mysterious Ways

Beth S. Wilson

I had the best job in the whole world. I worked there for almost ten years and I intended to spend my last sixteen years working at this same job. My bosses were incredible. They let me do my work. I had a voice when I needed one. My assistant was awesome. Life was good.

Then, they gave part of the company to the applications engineer. He was apparently very threatened by my position, because he shoved his weight around after that. Where I once could work without being told what to do, he now insisted I complete his project even though the deadline was eight months out. At one point, he even convinced one of the other owners that I had wronged him. I lost my voice! It's a horrible thing to have a voice and lose it.

But, I am a strong person. I wasn't going to let some insecure weenie threaten me.

In February, all the guys went fishing. Being a woman, I wasn't invited. It was okay, I really didn't want to go. Except, everything changed after they bonded over dirty fishing worms and beer. No one spoke to me. I became invisible. I don't do invisible well; I never have. They worked around me and went to my assistant. I did the best I could until June when I decided I would start looking for another job.

One Monday, I had a book signing to go to and I took a day of vacation. My boss called me and asked me if I was out looking for work. I immediately felt convicted by the Holy Spirit; if I said no and then found another job, it would look like I had lied to him.

I was told to start training my assistant to take over my job. Some days I panicked. I was training someone and I didn't have another job to go to. At some point, I decided I didn't want to leave anymore: I was that scared!

Sept 30, 2015 my boss called me into the weenie's office and told me it was time.

He let me go on the last day of the month. I haven't told you yet, but I have multiple sclerosis and my medicine is $4100.00 per month without insurance. To let me go on the last day of the month meant the very next morning, I wasn't insured. Our company was small, cobra wasn't offered.

It took a month of wallowing in self-pity, with no direction, pleading to God for answers. All I heard was, "Wait. Be still." I looked for work but couldn't stand the idea of being in an office again; the mere thought of it made me nauseous.

In the meantime, I had been dreaming of starting a publishing company. I had published my own book and one for a lady in my critique group. I was also working on edits for a friend of a relative, Mo. And I had two ladies under contract. But I was l scared to take the plunge.

Mo emailed me and asked when I was going to quit my job and start publishing full time. I told her I had been laid off. Her exact words, "How exciting you got fired!!!!! WOW if that isn't God speaking to you about what direction to go!!!!!!!! That makes it clear as it can be! Good for you! Sometimes that is what it takes to get us out of our 'secure' places to go be a warrior for HIM. Congrats!"

That was not how I was feeling, not at all, but she offered me a clear direction when I had none.

We met two days later and Mo gave me a gift. It was a check for the maximum she could write and it still be considered a gift.

Praise God, Praise God, Praise God!

She gave me another gift besides the check. She said she wanted me to invest into someone else's life when I got established. Right now God is preparing someone to receive what Mo has asked me to pay forward and I am excited beyond words to see it unfold.

The Publishing company Hear my Heart Publishing LLC, was created and I look forward to spreading the words God lays on your heart into all the world.

His Way is the Best Way

Darlene Shortridge

Co-owner of 40 Day Publishing

It is obvious by the following true life story that I believe in transparency. For the record, I am telling this story with my daughter's permission.

My heart felt as if it had been physically torn from my chest—beating, bleeding, and breaking.

The single most important thing in my life, next to my relationship with my Lord, is my family. My husband and I have two children, our daughter, Jonna, is the oldest and our son, Jeremiah, came ten years later.

As a Christian mother, nothing would make me happier than to have both my children grow up in their faith having never felt the need to venture out into the world. Sometimes that is not to be. There comes a point when our children must make their faith their own. Riding on their parents' coattails of faith will no longer cut it.

Our children were raised in the church. They know the who, what, when, where and why of almost every Bible story. I remember how Jonna was in youth group; the leader would ask a question and she would wait to answer, giving the other kids a chance to give the correct response. Finally, after listening to wrong answer after wrong answer, she would share the correct response. That never won her too many popularity points with the kids in her youth group! The Word had been as instrumental in her survival as her first breath. She grew up knowing the importance of faith to our family.

Jonna was a good kid. She was inquisitive. Downright nosy, really. She was also a bit sneaky. She never got into much trouble. The two times she got into big trouble were when she gave out her personal information on the internet, and when she purposefully hid the fact her cell phone had been taken away during lunch in high school. She hoped the notice came after the birthday party sleepover she was having. For the record, it did not and her party was cancelled.

We were strict parents. We meant what we said and we did what we said we would do. She knew this. She would tell her friends, "No, you don't understand. My mom will really do it." Therefore she kept her nose pretty clean all through high school.

Graduation and being of age brought a few bumps and bruises. After recovering, she decided she wanted to go to college and get her life moving forward. I really thought the worst was behind us. Not so. She found her freedom in the college scene. I routinely questioned her and she routinely assured me she had not lost her faith, she did in fact still believe, but she wanted to see what the world had to offer. I was scared for her. *Truly scared.* I reminded her that Satan and the demons believed. What they did with that belief was the true question.

I prayed. I prayed a lot. Little did I know that I had no idea what praying really meant.

After a year and a half in college, Jonna decided she did not know what she wanted to major in, so she was going to temporarily leave school. About this time I received a phone call from her roommate, who was extremely concerned with Jonna's drinking as well as the man Jonna was in a relationship with. I questioned her yet again. I asked if an intervention was necessary.

"Mom, I'm fine. Really."

Again, I prayed.

Jonna came home for Christmas and I learned she was serious about the relationship she was in. She also commented that she wanted to move closer to us.

My ears perked up. I wanted nothing more than to have my daughter close to me, where I could keep watch over her. If that meant she was bringing a man with her, well, it must be okay because surely God wants her home.

I picked them up from the bus station in February. We turned our office into a bedroom for our daughter. Her boyfriend temporarily took over our son's room. (Lesson learned: that will never happen again!)

We made every effort to get to know her young man and welcome him into our family. Our thinking was, if our daughter loves him then we must give him a chance and keep him close. The thought was akin to having our children's friends hang out at our house. We would be able to keep a closer eye on what was going on.

You know what they say about the best of intentions?

We began to notice things missing. For the first time in our lives, someone used our bank account to purchase something not approved by us. Items from our home started vanishing. Not only that, but he was also an excellent liar. I caught him on several occasions and called him on it. Every time we expressed our concern to our daughter, she defended him.

That was when she told us she was five months pregnant. I was stunned. In fact, I did not believe her, until she showed me the ultrasound. Although in shock, I remained calm. That was not supposed to happen. That was not in the plan. Our daughter was to go to college, get her degree, fall in love with a Christian man, and then give me the grandchildren I sorely desired. My plan went up in flames in seconds. A baby? And she hid the pregnancy from me for five full months! How could she?

Finally, he went missing. He reappeared days later. He had gone on a meth binge. That was who our daughter attached herself to. We were at a loss.

At this point, he was no longer allowed in our home. Our daughter was still strangely connected to him. He abandoned her, left her without a word and filled himself up on drugs, yet she still defended him. We could not understand.

Together they rented a house. She excitedly took me to see the house and although I tried to be positive, I could not hide the horror when I thought about my grandbaby living in such a horrid place.

We learned he had a warrant out for his arrest in another state. When he found out the police were looking for him, he told our daughter he would rather run than stay with her and support her and the baby. So, he left. He flat out told her he would choose evading the law over her.

We were out running errands when we spotted him sitting in a fast food restaurant. I called the police and within minutes they had him in the back of a squad car. My heart raced. I began to see the light at the end of the tunnel.

As we were driving home our daughter called. She told us her boyfriend had been arrested and asked if we knew anything about it. I told her yes, we saw him and we called the police. I had warned her beforehand if I ran into him, I would call the police. It should not have come as a surprise to her. She was frantic. She was sobbing. She left our home in an emotional thunderstorm. My husband and I looked at each other, knowing we did the right thing.

Shortly after leaving, my daughter called to let us know she just wanted to stay at her own house that night. I feared for her.

The heartache that comes from knowing someone you love is more concerned with themselves than with you or the child they conceived, is hard to cope with, especially when you are five months pregnant.

Fearing for our daughter's safety, we stopped by the house to check on her. The boyfriend had been released from jail and was back with her. She had welcomed him back with open arms knowing full well he would have left her and the baby without giving them a second thought.

To make matters worse, she had lied to me. I was confused, hurt, and I did not know what to do or where to turn. I felt as if my world was ending. I should have known God always has a plan, but sometimes it is hard to see the sun shining through the storm.

I sobbed my way through church. I could not stop. That night, I nearly did not attend life group because I could not stop crying. My heart truly hurt. I had no idea that a heart could hurt as much as mine did. I felt as if I had lost my daughter and grandchild in one fell swoop. I was grieving. She would not listen to reason.

We threw up our hands in defeat; we had tried everything! We had talked to her. We had him arrested. We fired her from her part time position with our company since we absolutely refused to provide any money for him to live on. Finally, I surrendered my control over to the Lord. I had exhausted every option—I had tried everything. Nothing I did worked. Nothing I did made a difference. She was still clinging to that man as if he had some sort of hold on her. If we allow the world or worldly influence to enter into our lives, indeed, the world will have pull in our lives.

Accepting the possible consequences, I stepped back and allowed God to take over. I gave Him complete control. If it meant losing my daughter and grandchild, so be it. I would just have to trust Him. And *believe*. Believe that no matter what happened He would work things out. He always does.

For the first time in months I was at peace. I knew that I surrendered my will and accepted His. I felt as if a heavy weight had been lifted off my shoulders. It is truly amazing when we hand our problems over to God, He really does takes them. I felt the stress, worry, and apprehension lift away like white puffy clouds drifting by with the breeze.

I began to seek God like I had never done before. I have never prayed like I did for that situation.

They were living with no electricity. No water. No screens on the windows. No refrigerator. No stove. They were going to the free local pool during the hot weather to shower. They had an air mattress and the table and chairs we had bought for her birthday. They had nothing else. He was fired from each job he had and didn't seem to mind having her fully support him while they lived in abject poverty.

I hated to see my daughter live this way.

As I prayed, I received very specific instructions on dealing with my daughter. We were to give them no money. We were not to enable them, at all. If my pregnant daughter wanted to come home for a meal or a shower, she was welcome. She was also welcome to come back at any time if she made the decision she would end the relationship. He was not welcome in our home under any circumstance. Period. The Lord spoke directly to my heart and said, *"If you listen and obey my voice, you will see your daughter's return."*

We heeded His instructions even though it nearly killed me to see the bug bites up and down her legs and the hurt in her eyes every time she came home.

I strongly felt I needed to fast. I began on a Monday and fasted through Saturday. On Sunday after church, my daughter came over and began to cry. She told me she wanted to come home.

The next day, we took our van and packed Jonna's things and brought her home. She has had no further contact with him and he did exactly what we expected him to. He left the state and has not taken any responsibility for his actions.

My daughter has continued to heal. She is living at home with us. We are closer than we have ever been. I continue to pray for her to find her way back to the loving arms of her heavenly Father. I see her making steps in the right direction and know that He is working.

I can honestly say that through one of the hardest years of my life, I also received one of the most amazing blessings of my life. My granddaughter has me wrapped around her little finger. I am simply enthralled with this child. She has the sweetest spirit. Her smiles light up my life. My daughter recently told me she wants her daughter in church every Sunday. I simply smiled.

God has been faithful through this whole ordeal. He continues to be faithful. He is worthy to be entrusted with our most coveted possessions, especially since they are really His, not ours. We are simply guardians to watch over them. We are to bring them up according to His plan and ready them for their part in furthering His kingdom.

If you are heartbroken over lost children, I am here to encourage you. God sees your hurt. He knows your pain. These are His kids, too. He loves them more than you and I are capable of loving them. Trust Him and listen to his instructions. Yes, those instructions can be hard to follow at times, but my story is living proof that heeding his voice brings direct results. He knows what is best. He knows how to get things done.

His way is the best way.

God Knows My Heart

Karen Forsythe

My husband, Steve, and I had just laid down to sleep Saturday, June 6th, a little after 11:00PM. The phone rang and it was Teri, Steve's ex-wife, on the phone crying. Through her crying, Steve made out that we needed to get to St. Francis as Sara, our daughter, was in a motorcycle accident. The police had visited Sara & Josh's neighbor who contacted Teri. Before he even hung up the phone, we were dressed and headed to the door. On the way, I googled "motorcycle accident Tulsa" and found a breaking news clip which included a photo. The picture was of a motorcycle accident at 53rd & Peoria showing an SUV with damage to the driver's side headlight area and a motorcycle lying down by the driver side door. The article read that the couple was hit by the SUV and the riders were ejected….the woman sustained severe head injuries and the male had an arm injury. Quickly, I dismissed this accident because if Josh had only an arm injury, he would have called us before now.

We arrived at the Trauma entrance and went to the information desk. Feeling frantic but trying to remain calm, my entire body was shaking as I asked, "Do you have a Sara Welch here? We were told she was in a motorcycle accident and she is here."

The woman, typing quickly, has a puzzled look and tries a different screen, again, typing quickly. "We don't have anyone by that name here."

"Are you sure?" I asked. "Try Josh Barnes. We were told that they are here. The police told us to come here." As she returned to her typing, the thought that they were dead crossed my mind and that's why she can't find them.

"I'm sorry," she said. "We don't have that person either. Let me check if they are in holding area."

Teri, Steve, Ryan (Sara's oldest brother), and I were bewildered and stepped away from the window. Ryan called his friend on the Tulsa police force to confirm we were at the right hospital. Teri and I talked about the Googled article and we both agreed that it couldn't be them.

Then, Ryan says, "Mark says that accident was them and they are here."

Immediately, I drop to the ground, praying, "Dear God, No! Please don't let this be! This can't be!"

Ryan says, "We have to keep it together." I jump up and return to the window and as if my new found knowledge will produce different results.

I say earnestly, "We were just told that they are indeed here. Can you look again?" This is when I see my brother has arrived, in his security uniform. He works at another Tulsa hospital and had been on duty at a street event where he heard about the motorcycle accident. How he knew it was our Sara I still don't know, but was glad he was there for me.

Someone came and told us that she was in room 326. I don't remember getting to the floor but I do remember the sweet, young trauma nurse who met us as we approached the door. She calmed us and walked slowly toward the door while saying, "Sara has suffered a head injury and we have made her comfortable." As she walks us into the room, she continues, "Sara's injuries are severe. Her pelvis is broken. Both arms are broken. And her x-rays show so many fractures that we cannot count them all. Her main trauma is her cracked skull. We have cleaned her up and stitched her head as best we can and covered that side of her face." We are crying, quietly, trying to hear something that would tell us she is going to be alright. Steve asks if Sara is breathing on her own. The nurse says, "No. The machines are doing the breathing for her. Her heart rate, pulse, and oxygen levels are good. Our concern right now is the brain swelling." The swelling is evident by Sara's one bulging eye that we can see.

Sara lay there, in the bed, as if she were but sleeping. We all are crying uncontrollably, hugging each other, and touching

Sara's arms or legs. Words being uttered- "This can't be." "She's a fighter." "We love you, Sara." More and more people began to arrive—Sara's siblings and childhood friends, Sara & Josh's church friends, our family and friends. Thoughts turned to the four-year old triplets that were sleeping soundly at Teri and her husband's home. Heartbreak upon heartbreak.

A couple hours later, the trauma doctor comes into the room. He re-explains everything the nurse had told us, but adds Sara most likely will not survive the type of head trauma she has suffered. Our hearts sink. Tears begin falling harder and faster. The doctor further explains that the head trauma and swelling is most likely impairing her ability to breathe on her own. Steve asks how long they will keep her on the machines and how will we know that she will or won't survive. With compassion in his eyes, the doctor matter-of-factly states that there are two ways to test her. One is to take her down to the room to test with some kind of injectable or they can take her off the breathing machine for 5 minutes to see if her brain will tell her lungs to breathe. If she doesn't breathe on her own, she will be considered brain dead. After a little discussion, we agree on the latter test. Steve asks when the doctor would recommend the test be performed. The choices—now or tomorrow. Unanimously, we chose "Tomorrow."

Around 4:30am Steve and I headed home to get refreshed. While Steve is driving, I had a vision. I turned to Steve, "I know you don't believe in heaven, but I just saw Sara there with Jesus. She better be getting instructions and come back because we need her!"

In the early hours of the dawning Sunday, the doctor approaches us about Sara being an organ donor should she not survive. He explained that the resident Donor Share Coordinator, Robin, would talk to us about the program and answer any questions we might have.

While we anxiously waited for the unassisted breathing test, we wanted everyone who wanted to see/talk to Sara to come before the test, as if she could hear us. Josh (Sara's fiancée) was still unconscious. His injuries were severe and he was on the same Intensive Care floor. While we were assured he would live, sadly, Josh would not get to say any goodbyes before or after the test. Although we had been waiting, it felt sudden when a different trauma doctor arrived. He explained the test and what he is looking for - chest movement and oxygen levels. Then he advised some may want to leave the room as it can be scary to watch with some reactions that could happen. I dared not budge! I remained at the foot of the bed, praying for God to heal her and let her stay with us. They shut off the life support and as we anxiously watched for any sign of her breathing on her own, the time passed as if in slow motion. The time lapsed and the nurse resumed the life support as the doctor declared time of death at 11:30am, June 7th 2015.

Grief overwhelmed everyone. Tears flowed. Hugs exchanged. Then thoughts quickly turned to the children she left behind. Not everyone would agree about everything but there were two things that all agreed upon; Sara's desire of donating her organs 'So others may live' and that her ex-husband would not be awarded custody of these small, precious lives.

My husband, the father of Sara, would become the main contact for the LifeShare coordinator at St. Francis, but all four of her parents and her sister, Hope, were taken to a family room to answer standard questions about our beloved Sara. Some were easy, others hard. As it sunk in, tears could not be stopped. We were actually discussing removing organs from our daughter. It was here that it began… we thought, "It just can't be real. It must be a very bad dream." These thoughts have been countless during the days and months that followed.

The LifeShare honored Sara's donations by raising a flag outside the entrance of the hospital. There was a ceremony scheduled for the next morning. The news media teams were there to capture it on film. You see five years earlier, they had broadcast a story about Sara giving birth to natural triplets and they were saddened for the loss too. Ryan, Sara's oldest brother, was chosen as the family spokesperson for the news teams. It was excruciating for him and yet he handled it quite well. Family and friends gathered for the ceremony. As it commenced, I am not sure what all was said. The feelings of grief and pride for Sara's choice felt at odds. But, knowing others would live provided solace.

Everyone handles loss differently. It is no different with organ donation. LifeShare provides the organ donor's family the opportunity to connect to the organ recipients, should both sides be agreeable about a year or so following the transplant. While Teri & Oscar (Sara's mom & step-dad) have decided to decline, Steve & I have expressed our desire to get to know the recipients. We look at it as a way to know how Sara's donations contributed to individuals, their families, and perhaps the world by extending their lives. In a way, it is Sara living on through others, kind of like we view her children.

Knowing Sara is with Jesus gives me a hope and a peace. I use this knowledge to temper the sadness. We all continue to fight our battles with grief, to remember all the good times with Sara and to find ways to keep her memory alive for her babies. But it works the other way as well; we hear Sara's laugh when Jayde laughs and we see Sara's smiling face when Jayde smiles. Jayde even thinks like her mother! It is soothing to experience those moments with Jayde. We know that there will not be Sara's reflections in the organ recipients but yet, we feel a connection with them all the same.

Open All Your Gifts

Lisa Bain

Joy In the Cause

    She would always say to me on our goodnight phone calls, "Lisa, have you opened up every gift under the tree today?" My Mom was wise. She taught me on the most difficult journey of our lives that the toughest days were precious gifts in disguise. How is that even possible with a diagnosis of stage 4 cancer, and my diagnosis the same week, of two autoimmune diseases? I was told to put away my running shoes and call it a day. Mom's prognosis was grim as well. On her worst day of hearing bad news from both sides, she sat up in bed and said, "Let's make this journey about *joy*! Let's help people through it and bring smiles where there are none. Let's see this as a gift from God! If we look for miracles we will find them!" She was right.

    Our trips to chemotherapy appointments became a party. From chicken suits to wearing disco wigs and funny hats, we spread joy. We laughed. We made precious friends. We sang songs. We listened to stories. We began to realize how much these patients needed *joy*. Some needed simply to know they had a cheerleader, and they were not alone. Our trips to spread joy grew into the desire to help spread joy to the entire community. Our biggest healing came from giving. Mom always said, "Giving=Joy, Joy=Hope, and Hope=Healing". She had it right every time. We wanted to share it all, so others could receive the same joy and healing we received. Joy In the Cause became a 501c3 nonprofit charity in September of 2013. The laughter continued with our tutu clad therapy leader being an English bulldog named Mavis Pearl. The last five years have been a miracle. Mom and I have a favorite verse, Jeremiah 33:3 "Call to me and I will answer you and tell you great and unsearchable things you do not know." We found those unsearchable things and great miracles we never dreamed. We found laughter on some of the darkest of days. We learned more than ever that what you see is what you are looking for, and to look for those miracles every day. We always found them.

Joy In the Cause has grown miraculously. Our mission is to provide care, compassion and joy through one personal act of kindness at a time. We deliver care packages that meet individual needs. We help those with any life altering illness and their families. It could be with a money card or gas card, house cleaning or a visit from Mavis Pearl; it could be a stuffed Mavis Pearl dog, decorated and dressed by hand, sent out with a prayer and blessing or simply just sitting with a patient on a chemotherapy appointment. Whatever is needed, we bring it with joy and laughter.

The miracle stories are endless. We have sent out over 4500 stuffed Mavis Pearl blessing dogs since we began this journey a little over a year ago. We have a village of volunteers that help dress each one and help with deliveries. Daily, God shows us unsearchable things we never dreamed and that only He could bring to pass.

As I look back at all those gifts under the tree that I never opened until this tough journey, I thank God I have opened them all now. Indeed, some of the gifts I left unopened turned out to be my biggest blessings. Had I not opened the box that contained cancer and autoimmune disease...oh the blessings I would have missed! God turned that box into a miracle, and my life has forever been changed because of it! The pair of running shoes I was told to put away was ten pairs of running shoes ago and the running continues! Have you opened up all your gifts? Merry Christmas!

It's Christmas every day.

Ten Years of Jehovah Jireh

John and Deborah Butler

Christ's Food Center

John and I opened a food center in the Kiamichi Mountains. Jobs were few and food was scarce. We felt compelled to feed the hungry the best way we knew how. We would offer the local people the word of God and enough food for a week. It wasn't actually enough but it was all we had.

We served in this ministry for ten years and have some wonderful memories that we would like to share with you.

2004 Favorite Memory

It was our first Christmas Eve at Christ's Food Center. There were no walls inside, no plumbing and very little electricity. We had been open only two months. The costumes, songbooks and even the life-like baby in the wooden manger were ready. At 7 pm Christmas Eve, the program began with a room completely dark except the light of a lone candle with three wicks (representing the Father, Son, and Holy Spirit in one God). I started with John 1:1, "In the beginning was the Word, and the Word was with God, and the Word was God." We alternated scripture readings and singing the carols that celebrated the events in the birth and life of Christ. First the angel's, then the shepherd's, then the king's, then the audience's candles were lit. There was a moment when we all stood up to bask in the room's candle glow and we sang "Oh Come All Ye Faithful." It was a very unifying moment. Everything faded except the beauty of the moment. There were no denominations, no boundaries, no prejudices, no rich, no poor, just people who had joined together to love God and praise him.

2005 Favorite Memory

We wanted to make sure our Food Center focused on spiritual food, not physical, so we started a mid-week Bible class. Our dear friend, Oma Hazen, attended every Wednesday night. One especially balmy summer night, the room was almost empty when she got there and without hesitation she got on her cell phone. We heard her strong country accent saying, "I'm here in Bible class-where are you?" Each person gave his or her reason for not coming. She responded, "Quit making excuses and come to Bible class!" And they came! She was able to say and do those things because she loved people. We lost her in 2007 to cancer. Her love and kindness still impact our community. We have learned to never underestimate a person's influence.

2006 Favorite Memory

Pride and self-worth come from sharing what we had, and having it valued, especially since we were poor. So when a truckload of donated clothes came, we considered a clothes ministry. The next day another truckload of clothes came. Clearly, God was putting a clothes ministry in our path.

We had no space in our tiny building for clothes so we judiciously kept only the ones that were new or like new and stored them in bins in our dining room.

We had two special Clothes Days that year. Each demanded the work of washing, storing, unloading, labeling, sorting and hanging hundreds of clothes. The shear physical work of it was enormous. Was it worth it? *Yes*! On the second Clothes Day, an 18-year-old girl came to look for jeans. She had dropped out of high school and run away to the city for a year, living on the streets. After coming home, she said if she could get some jeans, she'd go back and finish high school. She found five pairs of jeans in her size and five shirts. It was a moment when we saw

God's hand at work. Someone donated jeans they could no longer wear and God provided what His child needed to change her life- it was beautiful.

After she graduated, her family moved away and she married and had three children. We have learned to never limit God.

2007 Favorite Memory

We wanted to provide a place for people of all faiths to come together and worship God, so we decided to offer a worship service on Sunday morning and have food distribution after lunch. No one had to attend worship to receive food. We had thirty three puppets and four dedicated teens to be puppeteers for Children's Worship. It was fun! All ages attended. It was a joy beyond words to look out and see sixty people crammed into our little building, simply because they wanted to worship. One of our senior citizens was a rough-looking lady with multiple tattoos from the 1960's. She had no church experience, so every story and every song was new. It was amazing to see her transformation after she was baptized.

I can close my eyes and see her singing, "I have the joy, joy, joy down in my heart," with the enthusiasm of a child who loves God.

2008 Favorite Memory

We both love old movies. We wanted to provide wholesome entertainment for all ages every Friday night and make new connections in our neighborhood. The Big Cedar Movie Club only lasted one year since the license to show movies was expensive, but it was fun. The Talihina newspaper did a wonderful job advertising the movie each week. People brought their own snacks. The chairs were hard and the TV was small, but we all had a wonderful time. We met some very enriching families that never came to receive food, but were a blessing to us. One night we saw the movie "Ma and Pa Kettle Take a Vacation" and we had a room filled with people laughing. The warmth of some of these friendships remains dear to us. We have learned to never underestimate friends.

2009 Favorite Memory

Friends of Christ's Food Center joined together to give nine children a Christmas to remember. It had been a year filled with deep disappointment and discouragement for us, so we jumped at the chance to do the shopping to make these kids smile. It was the week before Christmas and in our living room we had nine huge piles of gifts. Each were purchased from the child's wish list and each were filled with extra clothes, bedding, shoes and coats appropriate for the child's age. We could smell the oranges, apples, candy, and other treats in the stocking.

We learned that even in the darkest times, there is a way to have joy, when you help a child know God's love.

2010 Favorite Memory

After we got the 501c3 status we received some amazing donations. That was the year of our best menus. One month, each family received eggs, hamburger, chicken, ham, bread, crackers, cookies, spaghetti, dry milk, oatmeal, juice, cereal, canned goods, fresh potatoes, apples, and tangerines. There was one skinny, scruffy looking man in particular. He was the sort of man who would not normally come for help, but his neighbor brought him anyway. He was hungry. His hand shook when he picked up the peanut butter. And he shed some tears when he signed out. Without a word, we knew he had been touched by God's kindness and love.

Sometimes we know we have done the right thing. We have learned that God has spiritual banquets prepared, but often it takes a neighbor caring enough to drive someone to receive it.

2011 Favorite Memory

As the number of families grew, we could not financially maintain a quality menu so we had to decrease our service area.

We asked the Community Food Bank mobile truck to come and provide food to help families make the adjustment. It was a beautiful, but cold, sunny February day. We had twenty seven volunteers that directed traffic, prepared food bags, escorted people through the process, received and carried food to cars and prepared lunch. In all, 102 families drove here and received food. At one point in the day, I stood back and saw a glimpse of what it would be like if all the Christians in our valley worked together to help people in need. It was beautiful!

I will never forget it. We have learned that people need strong leadership to accomplish great things.

2012 Favorite Memory

John was a computer technician before we moved to Oklahoma and he enjoyed refurbishing and repairing computers.

When two men in our community died in 2009 and no one missed them for weeks, I became more aware of the isolation many face here. That's when we began giving a computer to anyone that needed one. Many seniors became connected to family and friends. School dropouts connected to online schools.

One special memory for me was being able to give forty one computers that were donated by other non-profits in Oklahoma and Texas, to be used in various computer classes for orphans and abused women.

God gives us talents and we experience joy when we use them to glorify him. That is why Jesus said, "my burden is light". We have learned that the Holy Spirit is supposed to fill us not drain us.

2013 Favorite Memory

I will never forget the last night of voting in the Facebook Walmart grant competition. Chicago, Dallas, Los Angeles, Denver, Washington and other huge cities had great programs and lots of Facebook "friends". World-wide voting is out of the scope for rural Oklahoma. Yet, we witnessed a miracle!

Christ's Food Center came in 59th place and therefore received a $20,000 grant for a one year Food-4-Kids program. I smile when I think of it.

Every backpack was a blessing. There was one single dad in particular that touched my heart. He told me how he and his son sat down on Saturday night every week and did the Bible activity in his backpack. He said they had both had heard about the Bible, but had never read it, so together they discovered what is in the Bible. His son shaded the pages of the pencil book and the father read the words. Of course, that led to giving the dad a study Bible on Family Food Day. We have learned that often one event leads to another.

2014 Favorite Memory

Thanksgiving was beautiful. We served thirty eight families groceries for a bountiful Thanksgiving dinner. We have heard the horror stories of food centers that *stay open,* but give the hungry only rice, beans and old bread. We wanted to reflect the quality, integrity, and accountability worthy of Christ's name for the past 10 years and we have done that to the end.

As we finished this work in Big Cedar we have a profound sense of thankfulness to God. We learned God's sense of timing and his supreme wisdom as he opens and closes doors of opportunity.

We never forgot our real purpose and our real joy was to spread the good news: God is real, the Bible is true and Jesus is the Son of God and our hope for this life and the next. We tell everyone, "Read the Bible for yourself and do what it says. Love the Lord with all your heart and your neighbor as yourself".

Numbers 6:24-26 NIV
"The LORD bless you and keep you; the LORD make his face shine upon you and be gracious to you; the LORD turn his face toward you and give you peace."

The grace of the Lord Jesus Christ be with you.
Thank you for the memories!

We Gave it our Best Shot

Bridget Johnson

I met Chris when we were fifteen years old. It was absolutely love at first sight for both of us. The chemistry and feelings for each other were incredible. He was going to a Military School in our town due to the fact he was in trouble with the law in Oklahoma, so his parents sent him to Missouri to straighten him out.

Chris ran away from the school in April. He told my best friend as he left, "I love her too much to take her where I'm going." I was absolutely devastated. I went on to marry but still loved Chris the whole time. I committed my life to Christ on January 4, 1981. I told the Lord I wanted two things the day I got saved, to have a baby or take the desire away, and to see Chris again so I could tell him about the Lord.

Throughout the years I would ask the Lord if I could find Chris and He would say "No." However, many times the Lord would say, "Pray for Chris right now." Sometimes the intercession was so strong I would double up in pain. It happened many, many times from January 4, 1981 until I found him in April 1995.

On April 1, 1995 my husband and I split up and the Lord told me I could now find Chris. I knew he lived in a small town in Oklahoma and I knew his family were wealthy land owners. I tried to find the Chamber of Commerce in that area, thinking his family might be a member. It turned out the town was so small they didn't have a Chamber. I called the Town Hall and I spoke to someone Chris had gone to school with. The girl said she heard he was divorced and his family was living close by.

My best friend ended up talking to his step-mother. She said Chris was in prison for a year due to drugs and alcohol. I knew Chris struggled with that in high school so I wasn't surprised. She gave me his mailing address.

I knew his birthday was about the middle of April and Easter was very late that year. I mailed Chris a birthday card and an Easter card. In about a week, I heard from him. He remembered me and he received the birthday and Easter card on his actual birthday. Just that day he told the Lord "I want to serve you, but I can't do it alone."

For over a year I corresponded with Chris. During that time, he would tell me stories about how he should have been dead many times over. He would find himself high or drunk, he would wake up and not know where he was. I truly believe when the Lord said, "Pray for Chris right now," I was actually praying for his life to be spared.

I desperately wanted a chance to tell Chris about the Lord and possibly build a life together. Unfortunately, Chris was sentenced to 20 years in prison. He couldn't sell out to the Lord. He couldn't do it. I had to end the relationship.

I told the Lord I couldn't stop loving him on my own and He was going to have to take it away. One day as I was taking a walk with my best friend, I told her my love for Chris was gone. It felt as if it had been stuffed inside a helium balloon and sent up in the air, never to return.

I have memories of him sometimes, but mostly I remember he didn't choose the life God had for him.

The Lord and I gave it our best shot, but we still have our own free wills.

Hearing God's Voice

Bridget Johnson

Story two

My sister-in-law and I were pregnant at the same time. About September/October the Lord spoke to me and said, "Julie's baby is dead. Pray for it to come back to life and pray for her healing." I prayed until I knew I had broken through to Heaven.

Several days later, my mom called to tell me Julie had been diagnosed with leukemia and the baby hadn't moved in several days. I told her that Julie and the baby were fine, not to worry about it because they were healed. My mom, not a Christian, was livid because I wouldn't go to church and ask for prayer. I just couldn't. I knew it was already done.

Julie went to the doctor, the baby started moving (she's an adult now), and the diagnosis of leukemia was false.

God spoke and asked me to pray I am thankful I was listening.

Yes Lord

Judi E. Grove

Missionary to Kenya

I was a resident of Tulsa for the first 29 years of my life, until my husband, myself ~~I~~ and our children moved to Meru, Kenya. We received the Macedonian call at church. I had a burning in my heart during the service to become a missionary. My husband Bob, during the last hymn, leaned over to me and said, "I think we are supposed to go to Kenya."

I replied, "Yes, Bob, we are."

A year later, and half a million dollars had been raised to build a seminary. We packed up our three children, ages 11, 8 and 5.

The Bishop of Kenya was the instructor. The bunkhouse had room for 32 men. Conference and class rooms were built. It was my job to teach them how to use the flushable toilets. The conditions were poor. Everything including mixing concrete and washing clothes was done by hand.

The water came out of the jungle and had to be boiled and filtered. Boiling doesn't kill everything. There were lots of parasites.

At the end of the second year, I caught malaria. It was a four-hour trip to Nairobi to get medicine on curvy, bad roads. They were low on Quinine so I gave it to my children. It took four days to get more medicine and I was very sick. It took three more months in country before we could get back to the states. Then it took another six months before my health improved.

The seminary is in operation today and many people have been saved. We were obedient to God!

Once a Missionary Always a Missionary

Judi E. Grove

Story two

In 2007 I had a scare with breast cancer. My great grandmother and great aunts all had breast cancer, so while it turned out to be vessels that grew together and not cancer, it was still a scare. Because of my scare and my family history, I created Breast Impressions. We sent out plaster kits to ladies so that they could make impressions as a memento.

As a recipient of the 2010 Tulsey Award for Civic Entrepreneur, due to my breast cancer nonprofit work, I felt I should be doing more for all local people affected by *any* form of cancer.

While sharing my work with breast cancer fundraising, I was approached many times by local people who shared 'no one does anything about my (type of) cancer'. They shared they suffered from ovarian, prostate, brain or colon cancer, etc. Turn Tulsa Pink started after I had a dream.

On February 2, 2011, I dreamed I was walking in downtown Tulsa toward the BOK Tower, dressed in a pink wig, tutu, and pulling a wagon. People were pouring out of the downtown businesses and following me. I looked down at the pavement and the black asphalt suddenly turned pink! I looked up and the BOK Tower was pink. I sat straight up in bed, woke my husband and told him I knew that I was to Turn Tulsa Pink – not just for breast cancer, but for ALL men, women and children affected by any form of cancer!

PINK is the color of Passion, Power and Love – not just one cancer ribbon color. We are the all-inclusive Pink! I shared the vision with the Tulsa Community, and within months, hundreds of caring Tulsan's got on the 'Pink Band Wagon'.

When God lays a ministry opportunity at your feet, it is easy to see the finger of God working out all the details.

Miracles

Debbie Noble

A family is disconnected by infertility, anger, and hopelessness. A dad is searching for true and lasting peace. A younger sister mourns over mental health issues and financial struggles in her family. The finger of God can take all of these disconnected pieces and weave them into a beautiful tapestry bringing joy and happiness.

Twenty-four years ago, I experienced an ectopic pregnancy that landed me in emergency surgery while living in a foreign country. We were teaching for the Department of Defense Dependent Schools in Germany on a two-year contract. My husband and I had gone to the military hospital in the middle of the night, as I felt poorly and was having trouble breathing.

The ER doctor quickly determined I was experiencing a tubal pregnancy and immediately called the OBGYN on-call to my room. My blood count was only four and I had been bleeding internally for some time. Surgery had to be done immediately. The nurses and anesthesiologist rushed to prep me for surgery. I had lost so much blood that my veins were collapsing. It was difficult to find somewhere to put the IV tube. Finally, they had to put it between my toes. My husband was calm, but I could hear the concern in his voice when he told me "I love you," as they rolled me into surgery.

God IS good; the surgery was successful. I was alive. My husband and I were full of gratitude that I was given a second chance. We were saddened about the loss of the baby, but were given hope that becoming pregnant again was a possibility.

After a year of no pregnancies, we went back to the doctor and discovered our chances of having our own children were slim. Not impossible, but slim. We would have to undergo fertility treatments and even then, the possibility of another tubal pregnancy remained.

Wanting a baby with all my heart, I began researching adoption agencies, both foreign and domestic. Discovering the multitude of paperwork, fee and wait time, I became discouraged. I thought becoming a mother was one of the most important things that God has wanted for me to be. "Was this *not* His plan?" I kept asking...

During this time, many men who were serving in the first Gulf War were returning and starting families with their wives. Excitement filled my heart for these men who came back healthy and safe. Military wives, that were my friends, were now having children and building their families. Surely, God wanted that for me too. I was discouraged, but I knew my time for a child would come soon.

More discouragement continued. Romanian adoptions that had been open were now closed. A trip to Poland with an interpreter led to more closed doors. Russian adoption costs were astronomical. Many U.S. adoption agencies wanted large amounts of money with no guarantee of a baby. Two years had passed and still no child.

During a summer trip back to our home in the states, we found a Christian adoption agency in the Kansas City area. The fees were reasonable and we wanted to know more. We went for an interview and were accepted to be on their waiting list. It was a ray of hope. There were a lot of paperwork and special requirements, but the hope of getting a healthy baby was enough to keep us going.

Working on completing the paperwork, getting special recommendation letters and completing questionnaires was a lengthy process, but we were diligent and determined.

During this time, my dad lost his job just five years short of retirement age. It was a devastating blow to the whole family. He was a self-made man and did not have a relationship with God. He and my mom had to make some major financial adjustments while my dad decided his next career move.

My youngest sister began having some major marriage issues and it was difficult to see her in such agony. It was painful to watch her struggle with a husband who was bi-polar. Plus, he felt that doing drugs was the answer. My sister was strong but her family was paying a high cost.

My heart was full of concern for my family members. I felt the need to pray that God would make Himself evident in each family member's life.

I cried out to God, "More than wanting a child, I want all my family to know you on a personal level." I meant every single word. That moment, I decided that if I never had children, I would delight myself in praying for the rest of my family.

It became evident to us that moving back to the states was the right move for us. I began missing my family terribly and wanting to be closer to them. There was a great need for God to intervene in all of our lives.

The fall before we were to move back, my parents visited us for two weeks. My dad had started a new business that led him to making contacts with friends of ours in Germany. One of the friends was an American pastor starting a German Baptist church in the town where we lived. During his visit, our personal friend began talking to my dad about God. Remarkably, my dad was listening, or at least being polite. I thought my dad would reject the notion of becoming a Christian, but I kept praying. This could be a God-thing.

After helping with the new business contacts and some time for travel, my parents were on their way back to the states. Our pastor friend had left a book he thought my dad should read about knowing God. As we were gathering luggage to load my dad picked up the book and looked at it. "I think I might read this on the plane," my dad said. My jaw about dropped, but I knew God was working.

Two months after returning to the states, I received the most amazing phone call from my dad. He had read the book on the plane, considered it and turned his life over to God. He admitted that he felt a peace unlike anything else he had ever experienced. What a celebration phone call. I did a somersault!

The change in my dad was evident. Other family members recognized the change and they began to see the need in their lives as well. My younger sister and her husband began going to church and making a commitment on their family. My youngest sister recognized her need for God and started attending a church with her two young sons. Soon, her husband started going as well.

That June, we moved back to the states. My husband landed a teaching job in a small town outside of the Kansas City area. We found a lovely church filled with caring, praying people.

The following spring we received a call from the adoption agency. There was a birth mother who really liked our profile. Would we consider a Hispanic-American baby? Absolutely!

Five days later, we drove to Kansas City. Our case-worker took us to a foster home and we met a 3 week-old infant boy. We fell in love with him the moment we saw him. Our case-worker put the baby in our arms and snapped a picture. We were grinning from ear to ear! The foster family was wonderful. They even let us spend the evening with them, thus getting to spend more time with the little baby.

Three weeks and we would get to bring our little guy home. Frantically, we bought the necessary things needed. We drove to Kansas City the next weekend to spend time again with our future bundle of joy. The following Friday morning, we loaded all the necessary baby items and headed to Kansas City to bring our baby home.

First, we went to court to become legal guardians. The proceedings were quick and we were on our way to the adoption center. My whole family, along with our son's foster family, joined us for the ceremony. The director of the adoption agency asked my mom and dad to ring the bell tower, letting the city know that another abortion had been prevented.

The official adoption took place nine months later. Again, our families joined us to celebrate. The judge who declared the adoption final had the same name as our son. That Sunday was Easter and our son was dedicated with infant baptism. What a joyous occasion!

The finger of God was definitely working in my family. Only our God could work His plan and show us details that earmarked His handiwork. Our son is the only grandson that is adopted. Yet, he is the most like my dad in personality, drive, and personal preferences. We remarked about how only God can make all things work together for our good. God did more than we could ask or think.

Since the adoption, my mom and dad became missionaries. They travel the country helping others in need. My dad says that serving others and showing them Jesus is the most important thing in life.

Our family gatherings include prayer, fun, and lots of love. A smile came to my face the last time we were all together at my parent's church. The finger of God had taken all the disconnected pieces of brokenness in a family and weaved them into something beautiful and fulfilling.

Lessons Learned

Harold Bloom

My wife and I agreed to raise our children in a Christian church when we had our first child. The church did not understand the meaning of the word Christian as we later came to understand it. The word Christian means to be followers of Christ. In October 1980 I accepted Jesus as my Savior. *That is another story.*

In my twenties, I worked in the paint department at a plant that made aluminum siding. One of my co-workers was a very short man and had an attitude. I have always been tall and large. He wanted to fight me. I was ready, even though I didn't want to, but I needed him to leave me alone. This was before I had a personal relationship with my Lord. I finally told the man that I would meet him across street. I thought this would end the problem. Many people heard about the fight and came to watch. As the crowd gathered, my foreman stopped the fight before it even began. I didn't understand why the Lord came to my rescue.

I was told after the incident that the man had a steel plate in his head. I really don't know what the result would have been, but I may have killed him. I use this example many times as I teach the Scriptures to show we have choices to make. Good and bad, we can only hope the choices we make will be good ones and pleasing to the Lord. The man that wanted to fight me committed suicide about six months later.

I am thankful I was not part of it. Even before Jesus came into my life, He was watching over me. I believe He had greater plans for me.

***

After my wife and I retired, we traveled around the country and settled in Arizona for the winter. While we were in Arizona, we did some prospecting for gold. You can't begin to know how hard it is to find the elusive gold. While going off road, we would carry along our tools. When we found a spot, we would stop and do a little prospecting to see what we might find. What we're looking for in the desert is black sand or quartz. Gold can usually be found where these are.

After searching for those five years, we had in a little glass vial, about one fourth of an ounce. Not much for the amount of labor that went into finding it. But we had fun and it was exciting to find little specks of gold. It would make our heart beat faster. We had gold fever!

While traveling, I started having signs of heart problems. I had a small blocked artery the doctor treated with medication.. My sight had been hazy. After the medication the haze was no longer there. Can you believe it?

We decided to move back to Ohio. My son lives about an hour away from where we lived. We went over to his house one winter and I took the little vial of gold with us to show him. I put the gold in my pocket and on the way home we stopped at a restaurant to eat. I forgot about the gold in my pocket. After eating we left for home and I didn't think about the gold until about two hours later. It was not in my pocket. I headed back to the restaurant in hopes I could recover the vial. When I got there the restaurant was full of people at every table, including the one Judy and I had sat at. So I asked to speak to the manager and I told him my dilemma. He was sure, when they cleaned the restaurant, the vial would be turned into lost and found.

There were two men sitting at the table, probably businessman, well-dressed who seemed to be in a long conversation. The manager was reluctant to disturb these men and I understood. After a while, the manager came with a flashlight. He went over beside them and got down on his knees shining a flashlight around their feet looking for the vial.

The two men were surprised, as you can imagine, they wanted to know what was happening. I told them what we were looking for. The manager found the gold. I feel because of prayer and my strong belief, we found the vial and my heart went back to normal beat. I was praising the Lord for what transpired and how it ended up.

The labor that went into finding the gold was something we will never forget. We had more fun than an average person by going off road and searching for the elusive gold.

***

We decided to find a church close to our home. I wanted to start a men's breakfast as an outreach to other men. As the program started the Lord spoke to me and told me I must have testimonies and an altar call.

One Saturday, a man who was supposed to share his testimony, fell from a ladder the night before and could not be there. So I decided to share. While I was speaking I had chest pains and pressure. I was determined to finish.

The men that did the cooking were cleaning up. A man who had never been there before was washing dishes. I told the man I was having problems and needed to leave and the man asked me what was wrong. He stopped all the others from working and asked them to gather around me and place their hands on me for prayer. I immediately felt the presence of God and I knew I was going to be okay. Although others offered to help, I drove home and picked up my wife and we went to the hospital. Three stints were put in.

From this time forward, my commitment to the Lord became deeper. I asked God if I could be his clay and if He wanted to mold me. I told others about this and they told me that I needed to be careful what I asked for. I didn't understand: I was willing to be used by God.

Three months later the heart problems showed up again, and again the Lord was with me. Only one stint was needed and all was well. God was about to use me in ways I never thought possible.

Two people we met while traveling called and told me their mother died. They wanted me to perform a graveside service. They were un-churched and didn't want a pastor. My first thought was, "Me Lord?"

Then the Lord came back to me. "You told me you were willing".

Not knowing what to do or say, I started asking the pastors I know, and searching the internet. The answer always came back the same. Give them the bridge illustration and share the dash between birth and death, our lives here on earth. So I did and then I asked the people that were at the funeral if they had any stories to tell. The family told me they enjoyed the service and received comfort from it. I praised the Lord for giving me the opportunity, the strength and the words to minister to these people.

***

Another Saturday, the man who was supposed to come and share his testimony, at the men's breakfast, did not show. A little panic set in me. I asked one of the men who was supposed to speak the following month if he would share, but he wasn't ready. I went back to the table where I was eating. As I sat there a man approached me who had heard the conversation and told me that he started coming to the church in the last few months. He was convicted to be ready to share his testimony at a moment's notice. He told me he would be willing to share. I was elated.

The first thing he said was that he accepted Christ into his life in October 1980. It hit me in the head with a 2 by 4, because that was the same time I accepted Christ in my life. The message received from his testimony was that I was not in control. God would have whoever he wanted to speak at the breakfast. The goose bumps ran up and down my arms. There are times that I need to be reminded that it is not about me, but about God.

***

My father in law, Stan, was taken to the hospital. All kinds of tests were performed and they found there was a blood clot circulating in his heart. The family was called in. We had the opportunity to see the blood clot. It was unbelievable. The clot was looking for a place to escape by way of an artery. Then he would die.

The doctors were confused about to what do. They didn't have the proper facilities to handle the situation. The doctor asked what we expected. Judy and I told him "A miracle!." He decided to have Stan transported to another hospital. We knew the blood clot could move, and it would be all over. The doctor, for some unknown reason, decided to run the tests again. This time the blood clot had disappeared. He called for other doctors and they found nothing. Until this time there seemed to be no hope. The only things that had transpired, was prayer and a blood thinner. Judy, I and many from our church had been praying. The doctor said the blood thinner would take three or four days to help.

When the doctor told us what happened He said "It must be God." Judy and I agreed. After the doctors left we asked the rest of the family what they thought happened. They said the dumb doctors didn't have any idea what they were doing. They couldn't figure it out. But the truth was they didn't understand that God was involved. I wonder if they even prayed and if they had, would their prayers have been heard? To this day we know that some of the family has never accepted Jesus as their Savior. They tell us they don't want to hear anything about God and this grieves Judy and me. They don't understand or care where they will spend eternity. Our Lord doesn't want anyone to perish.

Stan went on to live another three years. We enjoyed the extra time with him and we'll see him again in heaven.

***

A pastor from our church was looking for help ministering to men with drug and alcohol problems. He asked me to teach one day a month. I agreed. The pastor was always there and I bounced ideas off of him.

Six months passed and the pastor felt called to another area. I thought I should step up my program, but I needed some clarification. I didn't want to confuse the men about the word of God. I went to the office and talked to their spiritual leader because there were some issues in their doctrine that I was taking exception to. He confirmed his beliefs were the same as mine.

I was told the men would either love me or hate me. If they hated me, I would no longer be welcome. After two years. I am still there. I have grown to love each one of these men. Jesus died for the forgiveness of our sins. I was always told I couldn't teach and the first day I was scared to death, not of the men, but that I might tell the men something contrary to God's word. But as I started to teach, the message became clear to me. God told me where to find a specific scripture and how to answer the men's questions.

I believe this ministry is flourishing because I am willing.

Healing from Above

Judy Bloom

I twisted my ankle while I was in x-ray technician training. The doctors told me I needed to go and have my ankle broken and reset. The thought horrified me and I chose not to have it done.

After Harold and I married the pain became unbearable and I decided to go to the doctor. He told me it was time to operate. It would be a three inch incision and a year of therapy. They would cut the tendon and tie it back together. I decided I had no other choice.

Some of our friends stayed with Harold during surgery. They prayed and waited for a word from the doctor. When he did show up he said there were some complications and it was the worst case of a sprain he had ever seen. He asked Harold what he expected and being a Christian he told him he expected a miracle. The doctor said the tendon were like strands of spaghetti. He said he had read an article about a procedure where a surgeon sutured the strands back together instead of removing a seven inch section. Harold approved.

After the operation they put a cast on my ankle up to my knee. I had it on for about four weeks. When I went back to have the cast removed, I couldn't believe it. The nurse asked Harold to come back to help settle me down. No one told me how much they had cut my leg and when I saw the scar it scared me. I didn't think I would ever walk again.

An appointment was scheduled for therapy in two weeks. When I returned, the therapist asked me to walk and he was dumbfounded at the totality of my healing.

The therapist called the doctor and he agreed that therapy was no longer needed. Remember, I was supposed to have a year of therapy.

As new Christians we saw this as a miracle and praised the Lord.

Too Close for Comfort

Beth S. Wilson

I was a single mom with no patience. One day traffic was busy in both directions. I wanted to pass the motorboat in front of me, but it was impossible. The girls were hungry and tired, and I was stuck. I would swerve out to see if the road was clear and would have to move back quickly to avoid getting hit.

I realized I was angry and out of control. I was too close to the boat, so I backed off.

As we were driving up hill, the motor fell off the boat. It hit the road and bounced right for my windshield. I screamed and scanned right, the ditch was too deep. I swerved left into oncoming traffic.

To my amazement, there were no cars. I was able to safely avoid the motor.

That day, in that car, God saved my life and the lives of my two girls.

Tears from the Heart

Penney Camper

I can remember the day it started. I ventured out of my protective bubble and into the world. My first day of kindergarten should have been exciting and fun, but instead, it was filled with emotion. I was fine until a little boy named Gary came into the classroom and burst into tears. He was scared and cried uncontrollably. I cried, too. I became overwhelmingly aware that the world was not filled with laughter, fun bedtime stories, dolls, little brothers and peanut butter sandwiches cut in triangles. There were kids who were sad, teachers who were mad, bullies and big scary school buildings that were easy to get lost in. No, my first day of school was not fun; it was the beginning of a long tearful journey.

Through my elementary school years, I cried. Each day was a different reason and usually I was not the victim. I cried because someone took my friends lunch. I cried because my teacher was sick and in the hospital. I cried because... the world was harsh and hurt people.

I cannot imagine what my teachers thought. It must have been difficult having the "crying girl" in their class or to be my brother, a couple of grades behind me, to be known as the brother of the "crying girl". I know it was difficult on my parents when the school would call and tell them "she's crying again." When asked, I could not really put my finger on the reason why, I just could not help it.

None of us realized I was overly sensitive to the needs, hurts, frustrations, and fears of others. For whatever reason I wanted to "fix it" for everyone. When I couldn't, I cried!

Those years of tears quieted as a teenager, but I was still very aware of other's needs. In a room full of teenagers, I saw a girl in the corner and gravitated to her. That girl's dad had committed suicide. I didn't know about her circumstances as I walked toward her, I knew something was wrong so I went over to talk to her. She needed a friend.

I sat in a classroom and did not hear a word the teacher was saying. I was often accused of being a daydreamer instead of listening. I was wondering why the teacher appeared to be troubled. I pondered what I should say to her to help her. I found out later that her daughter worked in a factory and her hair had been pulled into a press and scalped her. Thankfully her daughter was going to be okay, but this poor teacher was trying to continue teaching while at the same time wanting to run to her daughter. I grabbed her hands and told her I would pray for her and she wept.

In church, as I sat behind a friend, I noticed something was different. I could not explain it, but something was troubling her. The congregation bowed their heads for the opening prayer and I looked up just in time to see her slip out of the auditorium. I followed her, so that I could pray with her and talk to her. The first words out of her mouth were "how did you know something was wrong?" She and her husband were having marital problems and she cried as I prayed for her.

I am often asked how I know these things. I do not know, I *just do*. One of my coworkers calls me the office detective, I seem to hear and observe things even without being told directly. I do not do it on purpose, I have an awareness of the people around me. It helps me know how to pray for people or talk to them.

As I grew up, God helped me polish that sensitivity. I had a few skinned knees in my walk down the path God had placed me on, but through the years, the tears from the heart have grown into a heart for God's hurting people. It was not God's will for a little girl to spend so many years in tears, but I do believe he was molding my heart for a purpose.

At one point, I even fell into a toxic friendship. I sensed a need in this person and reached out to help her. I was still learning and did not mix the wisdom of God with the sensitivity He had placed in me. I let a bad friendship go on way too long. But the Grace of God was there to teach me in the midst of it and give me the strength to cut those ties. He also showed me how to be sensitive and pray for situations, but it doesn't always mean I need to get involved!

I still have times where I get sucked into a sad story and have to ask God for His wisdom to mix with the compassion I feel for others. I now work in a church office in the pastoral care department. I hear stories of hurting, sick and needy people. Daily I learn about God's love for those people. I look back and see how He prepared the heart of a little girl for this moment that I live in right now.

Jeremiah 29:11 Living Bible

For I know the plans I have for you, says the Lord. They are plans for good and not for evil, to give you a future and a hope.

Make the Connection

Penney Camper

Story Two

Through the years, I have been able to look back and see a divine connection has brought me to a place or decision, sometimes days or years following the connection. I have always believed that "Our steps are ordered of the Lord" Psalm 37:23. This past fall made that scripture find root in my heart.

Every year I fly from Tulsa to Colorado to see my parents. I usually gauge my arrival sometime in the late fall or early winter so that I can hopefully see a snowfall. I miss the Colorado Mountain snows so much and look forward to an annual visit.

This particular year, my trip planning kept coming up 2 weeks earlier than I normally do. While it meant that I could see the colorful changing of the trees from green to a beautiful golden yellow, it also meant that I would most likely miss the first snow. No matter how I tried to work it, the date kept coming up for the last week in September.

Fast forward to the airport. As I sat among the other travelers waiting to board the plane, out of the corner of my eye I saw an Asian Cowboy. He was rather short, had a canvas satchel around his neck to hold his travel papers and passport and had a big black Stetson cowboy hat on his head. His skin was dark tan, his hair as black as his hat and he had an ear-to-ear grin. I was quick to judge, wondering what type of person this was and giggled to myself thinking who would have to sit next to the Asian Cowboy. You guessed it! That would be ME!

At first, he sat with his shoulder turned away from me. He was pleasant, but quiet. Finally, I got the nerve to start up a conversation and I asked him if he was from Tulsa. He began to tell me that he is originally from Burma, but lives in Australia. He said he is a Pastor of a church in Australia and was in Tulsa to minister to other Pastors at a convention. At that moment, I wondered to myself which of us had been set up by God! I felt that one of us was about to hear a word from the Lord.

I told him that I worked for a church in the office as an administrative assistant to one of the Executive Pastors. He said he felt uncomfortable coming to the United States to minister to Pastors, especially in the Bible belt. He couldn't understand why American Pastors needed a missionary from another country to come to them. Shouldn't it be the other way around? He left a family in Australia to come here. He has 2 young daughters and a baby on the way. He hated being away from them and was beginning to question traveling to minister to other pastors.

The more I listened to him, the more I tried to tune in to God's leading. I felt like God wanted me to encourage him. I thought, "Ok, God caused our paths to cross so that I could encourage him." I proceeded to tell him that revivals are happening overseas! God is moving in other countries because of the people's hunger for the Lord. The United States churches have become used to the biggest and best, grand productions, rehearsed series' and need someone like him to remind them of the reason they do what they do. I could tell his heart for God was pure and real. I told him that I was not being judgmental or specific to any one pastor or church, but that I was sure that they needed what he had to give.

My cowboy friend asked if I would be willing to be his prayer partner and pray for him and his ministry. He said he was tired and prayed for a refreshing and that God had answered his prayer through our flight from Tulsa to Denver. He wanted someone to agree with him for wisdom. He wanted direction and confirmation that he is doing what God has called him to do. Just having another Christian to talk to that had the same heart was what he needed. He told me that he so wished that we could be on the same connecting flights. Unfortunately, he was going to Phoenix and I was going on to Grand Junction.

And then… God showed me that this was a 2 way divine connection. My travel companion said that I radiated God's joy and peace. He laughed when he heard my last name, loved the idea of being a "Happy Camper", and began to tell me that God had a plan for me to share His joy and peace with others. He asked me many questions about where I work, what my dreams are, and what my thoughts about certain things are and about the business my husband and I have.

I too was tired. I was reviewing my purpose, feeling ineffective and wondering if I was even making a difference. I also desired a change and wanted wisdom and direction as well. This Asian Cowboy reminded me that I do have purpose no matter what I am doing. He reminded me that I have joy and peace on the inside of me and that it ministers to others as I share and pray with them. I really do make a difference because of Jesus inside me!

The whole flight it was as if we were distant bystanders listening to our mouths talk and say things to each other that were spot on. The Holy Spirit had much to say that day. We talked about the scripture that says "As iron sharpens iron, so one man sharpens another." Proverbs 27:17. God choreographed our steps so that we would connect on a specific day at a specific time to deliver a message from the Lord.

When our flight ended, we walked off the plane in silence pondering what we had just heard. When we reached the open area of the airport, it was time to hurry to our connecting flights. The distinguished pastor put his black Stetson back on his head and grabbed a piece of paper to write. We exchanged email addresses and hugged each other. We had made a heart connection. We both promised to stay in touch and pray for one another.

I am more fully aware that God is a God of details. He is at work all over the world. To show His love, to deliver a word and to set answers in motion, he often needs our obedience; sometimes to be the deliverer, sometimes to be the recipient. Either way, I want to follow the steps he has placed before me and make the right connections.

God is Good

Susan Miller

Clinical Aesthetics of Tulsa

Summer is typically a slow time for the clinical aesthetics industry, and the first summer I was in business was especially slow. I was a new business, working to build my clientele while trying to get through my first summer. Money was tight because patrons were few and far between.

It was the last day of July that year and my rent and utilities were due the next day. I was short and didn't have enough money to make both payments. I prayed and turned the outcome over to God.

Late that afternoon, a lady called wanting a consultation for laser hair removal. She arrived at 3:00, two hours before closing. I went over all the information and she told me she wanted to get started. Not only did she want to get started, she wanted me to treat multiple areas.

I told her how much the total would be and offered her my customary discount if she wanted to pre-pay for the services. As it turns out, she did. Her total was $3000. She reached into her purse and counted out 30, one-hundred dollar bills on the corner of my desk.

My heart swelled and a huge lump came into my throat as I *knew* this was God's provision for me. And because God is who He is, He saw to it that she brought cash. I didn't have to wait for a check to clear. I could pay my rent and utilities the very next morning.

God is good!!!

Gifts From God

M.N. Morrow

Morro Bay enchanted me as a child. The sandy beach muddled with giant boulders and long weathered-wood piers made for exciting adventures. I was a small seven-year-old with an overabundance of imagination. I could often be found under the docks collecting starfish and shells. I would pretend I was a mermaid, "Nadia of the High Seas!" If I wasn't in the water I was on the pier people watching or interrogating the ship's crew about their last voyage.

I was a free spirit. I had tanned skin, wild hair that glowed like starlight and giant black-brown eyes. My clothes were always torn or too small and I would wear them for days at a time, often adorning them with long semi-fresh seaweed scarves. I twisted my hair around driftwood instead of barrettes. The other children usually made fun of me saying, in truth, how stinky I was and that I didn't have parents. The latter may as well have been true. I would daydream in class while watching ships sail away and long to be under the dock with my starfish friends.

At noon the other children would pull out their lunches and pile their desks with oranges and fluffy white sandwiches with toasty brown crust and other snacks that smelled so good. I would sit in silence trying to will my stomach not to growl, or ask to be excused so I could spend the time on the playground.

When the dismissal bell rang I was the first one out, charging past the perfectly dressed children strapping their back packs on, and their waiting parents.

I ran to the pier every day after school. I spent hours there until it was dark and I had no choice but to go home.

I took my time hiking up the hill to the row of townhouses where we lived.

I usually stopped and tried to catch the stray cats so I wouldn't have to go in alone. I managed to catch two in the six months we lived there. They were promptly put back outside once they were discovered, but it usually took a few days.

There was no furniture in the house and no decorations, except for the rocks in front that I sometimes left starfish out on until I realized they were meeting unfortunate ends. I was told that we weren't going to be there for long. Like every other place we lived, I was alone a lot. I never really knew where my mother or her boyfriend was and I was safer when they weren't there.

I stopped being scared one night when I left the window open and I could hear the ocean singing its lullaby's; from that night on, it put me to sleep.

My parents were almost always there in the mornings, crashed on a pallet on the floor. I would sneak past them and hurry to school for the free donut and carton of milk. I was never tired of eating that fried cake, dipped in sugar and cinnamon. I missed them when school was out for the weekend or there was a holiday. Fortunately, I learned how to distract myself during the day so I didn't care about food, unless I was playing downwind of the restaurant on the pier. I sometimes caught wind of the fried-buttery delights. The captain sometimes shared his food with me. I never begged or asked, or told him that I had not eaten for a few days. He just knew. I think God gave him that gift.

Hunger usually only bothered me at night when there were no distractions other than plush carpet, linoleum flooring, and an empty buzzing refrigerator that I sometimes cried myself to sleep in front of. I never knew how, or who, but I would be carried into my room and wrapped in a blanket and the pains would fade away. I imagined maybe God gave me an angel to stay with me when I couldn't find my mom.

I smile and feel a deep connection when I see the pictures and "Footprints in the Sand" posters. I know there have always been gifts from God in every day to shape me into the person he's designed me to be.

I can look back at all the tragedy in my life and take note of what could have happened, if God had not sent angels to help me.

Perfect Peace

Kerrie Tims

I received a phone call July 9, 2013, the day before my son's 18th birthday. The Nurse Navigator said, "I'm sure you have been waiting on my call." I told her I had and I knew what she was going to tell me. Somehow, I felt a peace and confidence that was clearly not of my own will. She asked if I could talk and proceeded to say that awful word no one ever wants to hear... CANCER!

A friend of mine had dealt with breast cancer a few years earlier and I was terrified for her. After praying for her, fear was still very real. I couldn't imagine what I would do with such devastating news.

Because of the Holy Spirit covering me with peace, fear has not been a factor in my diagnosis. The cancer walk has not been easy. I've had my share of surgeries, chemotherapy, radiation, nausea, fatigue, etcetera, but fear has not been on the agenda. The peace God has given me has been the biggest gift I could have asked for. Like He gave His son Jesus, without asking, He also gave me the gift of peace without asking.

I don't know for sure if I will have a reoccurrence of cancer or not. What I do know for sure is that God will be with me regardless of what the future holds.

How God Has Worked in My Life

Mark Berrier

I was asked some time ago to explain briefly on paper how God has worked in my life. I have written over 90 pages on my autobiography, and most of that explains God's work. How can I distill all that he's done for me into a brief story?

When I was 20 years old, God moved in me. I came to him a broken and sinful young man. I could not really believe he had forgiven me until I had been a Christian for 17 years. My sins were so great, mainly sins of the flesh, that I doubted I was worthy for heaven, let alone friendship with God. But when I was nearly 38 years old, I was told to read a part of I John, and where it said, "us" and "we," I was told to put my name there. I read: "By this Mark knows love; not that Mark loved God, but that God loved Mark and gave himself for Mark." When I read that, the universe seemed to lurch! It was like a quantum leap! I was forgiven. Jesus had died for me. The *doctrine* of atonement had been in my mind for years, but I had never appropriated it for myself until that time.

Suddenly, I knew God had forgiven me. Immediately after that, I was able to forgive myself. It was then that I stopped being so judgmental of others. I was free! I no longer felt lost. Finally, the teaching I had received over so many years had sunk in. I was a new man. I had finally *experienced* forgiveness.

Since that time, I have had three or four other "quantum leaps." It seems that 99% of the time the Christian life is one long plateau, but then something will happen that makes us jump way ahead of where we were. And then it seems we are back on the plateau again. My last "leap" was about ten years ago, when I suddenly understood the Hebrew language from the *inside*. I had taught Hebrew and Greek for more than 30 years when this happened. Greek is more like English, so I felt I understood it earlier, but Hebrew was another thing entirely. I was in a dark room when a light suddenly came on! I was surprised that I "got it."

I believe that the Christian life is a "long obedience in the same direction." If we continue in the truth, and continue studying and keep our faith in Jesus, God will at times drag us quickly forward. That is what happened to me.

God has provided me a wife, two children and 8 grandchildren. God has given me everything I needed for 74 years. I know he will ever stop. I praise him!

God's Timing

Jerri Ann Currey

Summer 1996

After four rounds with IVF during the first half of 1996 and ten years of marriage trying to grow our family, I was in the middle of the most stressful process I could have ever imagined. We argued so much and did not like being in the same room together those days. I wondered what my purpose was if I couldn't conceive a child and be a mother. If life wasn't going to give me this one thing, then why bother? Why bother with marriage, we did not even get along together.

Late Autumn 1996

After a few months of co-existing, I reached inside myself to the place that holds my faith. I had finally decided to give it to God. So I prayed, I asked God to grant us the opportunity to be parents one day. I really let go, giving Him the timeline. Then I went to work with my normal routine and felt truly released from my depressed state of mind. We were better together.

Three days after my prayer I received a phone call.

The phone call changed our life, it brought our daughter into our lives, made us parents, made all our dreams come true and that phone call was made by God.

I know he made Emma for us, regardless of the circumstances of her birth, she was always meant for us.

I am Healed

Bethany Duarte

Modern Day Wordsmith

In early 2014, God put a few different things on my heart: the word "discipline," the idea of having an "epic year," and a word that it was a "make it or break it" kind of year. As any planner does, I internalized those things and envisioned how I could see them playing out. I saw a version of myself after a year of being a dedicated boot camp participant, traveling to Vancouver on a spontaneous trip, coming home to sing with the worship team at Victory, and do it all with a newfound freedom (and a future husband, if it was a REALLY good year). To me, "epic" meant bigger, better, stronger and more full of life than ever.

Well…you know what they say about the best-laid plans…

It shouldn't come as a surprise to me that God always does things in ways we can't predict. Sitting here and looking back over the year, I can say with confidence, I may not have chosen the road God took me on this year, but I'm grateful that he did. I expected a certain type of "epic," but what was really epic was what God did *in* me.

My annual introspection changed in perspective after church in January when my pastor preached on personal highlight reels. When he mentioned looking back to thank God for all he'd done, it took me more effort than it should have to dig out of the negativity and defeat that had permeated my mindset. Once I was out of the mire, God began to bring blessing after blessing to my mind, little reminders of his faithfulness and his hand on me throughout the year. Not only did he remind me of the little gifts, but also of the battles, the wars, the all-out, drag-out American Ninja Warrior-style bouts I had with the enemy this year, because he was there too. He also reminded me of the scars, the wounds and the bruises that I endured.

On their own, they spoke the same message of difficulty that I had been picking up on. Merged together and placed on top of the year's themes of "discipline" and "epic," another picture began to emerge, one befitting of a highlight reel.

When I stopped to count my blessings, I could see how much I've changed by observing what I considered a blessing:

Taking the time to apply the right amount of blush and glittery eye shadow to my niece to go with her fairy ballerina princess costume.

Tearing up like a proud big sister as my "little brother" graduated from high school. Tearing up again when he let me know he got an A in English Comp at the end of his fall semester at OSU.

Laughing into the breeze when Pharrell Williams' "Happy" came on for the tenth time while I was driving along the California coast on a perfect, sunny day in my rented red mustang convertible.

Seeing God provide the money to pay my bills $5, $10, and $20 at a time until they were fully paid…never early, but never late.

The joy of seeing my freshly painted, signature mint green nails and realizing that color reflects the joy inside.

Seeing the first photo of my new niece, Miss Angelica Scarlett, and praising God for the little miracle that she is.

Freedom from insecurity, dishonesty, jealousy, comparison, anger, un-forgiveness and so many other chains that were holding me back from all God wants to do in and through me.

Witnessing three friends say "I do," before God, family and friends.

Finding a church where I feel right at home, where I'm constantly challenged to grow and to reach those around me and where the gifts God gave me have a place in bringing others to Christ.

Friends who stood, laughed, rejoiced, prayed, mourned and sometimes crawled with me through a season when I had very little to give in return.

A roof over my head, healthy food in my belly, clean water in my glass, and the perspective to know how big of a gift that is.

The list goes on and on. God was faithful to provide, to comfort, to forgive, to console, to challenge, to bless, to correct, to guide, to restore and to heal. He wasn't a Pez dispenser, giving me all that I asked for. Instead of spoiling me, he raised me. He gave me what I needed, instead of what I thought I wanted. It wasn't a year of plenty. Instead it was a year of learning to trust that what he provided was more than enough. It wasn't a year without suffering. Instead, it was a year to learn empathy for others that are struggling, and to give out of my own grief.

At the time, these lessons were not what I would call blessings; however, when I see the foundational changes in who I am and who I was, I can do nothing but thank him for knowing what I need even when I don't.

Some of the greatest blessings came through the fiercest battles. My pastor said something that really stuck with me. He said, "Battles are not always a sign that you've sinned or done something wrong; instead, battles tell you the Lord trusts you enough to make it through to the other side for his glory."

Looking back over the past 12 months, that knowledge changes the filter of the image from something grainy and grey, to a vibrant, full-color image befitting of an epic soundtrack.

I fought a battle against myself over my identity. When circumstances stripped me of all the things I had placed my hope and identity in, I was left feeling like a child again. God had offered to adopt me into his family, to take on the identity of his beloved daughter, but I had yet to accept it.

I received that offer of adoption by faith in August, 20 years after it was first offered. In my tears, I honestly told God that I didn't know what to do next and I didn't know how to move forward, but that I wanted him to move forward with me as my Father. I gave him my honesty and asked him to help me trust him.

And he has proven himself faithful, time and time again. He has provided for my needs, given wisdom when I asked, given comfort when loneliness knocked me on my back, given healing where there were hurts and most importantly for me, has been there for me through the ups and downs of the year. His perfect love chipped away at my old fears of abandonment, little by little. I admit, I'm learning what it really means to identify myself as a daughter of God, but what I do know is that before I'm a writer, a friend, or a future wife and mother, I am a child of God. And that I am complete in that alone. The rest is icing on the cake.

The battle that caused the most pain and simultaneously the greatest blessing was my fight against my own body. For someone who had never dealt with more than the occasional ear infection and strep throat, this was an eye-opening experience.

Health problems turned my life upside down. My independence turned into dependence in a flash. While I was grateful for a home to live in and someone to drive me places, I missed my adorable apartment and the ability to just up and go when I wanted to. I resigned from my job and it was one of the hardest things I've ever had to do. I gave up my source of income, financial security, a part of my identity, and let's face it…my pride…for a period of undetermined rest. It's not what any woman in her late-20's wants to think about or walk through.

While I have cried my fair share of tears about it over the past six months, and thrown myself more than a few pity parties along the way complete with sparkling cider and dark chocolate, the perspective and faith that have come as a byproduct have been worth every tear.

Life changed when I had to be very careful about expending my limited energy.

It changed when I had to watch what I ate very closely, avoiding allergens and doubling up on nutrients, all the while trying to fit into my old social scene as if nothing was wrong.

It changed when I realized that thousands of people live with chronic illnesses every day, and have dealt with them longer than I have.

It changed when I began to give God every decision before it's made, asking him for wisdom on even the smallest things because only He knows how it will affect my wellbeing in the long run.

It changed when I stopped viewing myself as entitled to good health because I'm young and invincible, and started treating my body like it's the temple of the Holy Ghost.

It changed my priorities when I was not guaranteed tomorrow.

It changed when my self-discipline determined how I felt one day to the next.

It changed when I choose to be around those who energized, challenged and sharpened me, and avoid those who drain, criticize or limit me.

It changed when my faith shifted from relying on what I see and feel, what aches and doesn't work as it should, and what the doctors say or don't say...to the unchanging God who healed every disease – the ones the doctors know what to do with and they ones they don't – two thousand years ago on the cross.

It changed when He becomes the Great Physician in more than just my Bible, but in my heart.

It changed when I realized that my circumstances have no bearing on God's goodness, but His goodness has the ability to radically transform my circumstances.

It changed when the limitations of my body stripped my pride and humbled me before the only one who can heal me.

It changed when healing wasn't an option, but a fact. It's already occurred and I got a smile on my face in anticipation of the day it manifests.

It changed when my answer in response to everything becomes, "It is well with my soul."

Sickness changed a lot of things. But what I allowed God to do with it was change me in the process. I thank God for strength to go for a walk now. My mealtime prayers are more than just formalities and moments of gratitude, but intense blessings over the food that God designed to support my body. I value every moment differently, knowing that they are finite, that the next one is not guaranteed, but a blessing from God.

While I still don't have a clear answer from the doctors on what my body is dealing with, God has given me his answer: I am healed. And while I am anxious to get back to being the healthy person God designed for me to be, I am so grateful for the things He has taught me and continues to teach me along the way.

He didn't bring the disease, but I thank him for allowing me to walk through it because the woman who is emerging trusts more deeply, takes nothing for granted, loves more fully and enjoys life without reservation.

Fear did play a role in this journey, as it often does with unknown health issues. For me, it was more than the fear of the unknown, but of what it would take to realize full healing. I know from experience that God can heal instantaneously, but he also uses doctors and medicines, and sometimes...he heals once the person has gone home to be with him.

I've always wondered how I would respond if the word "cancer" ever became a part of my vocabulary, or a possibility in my body. Recently, I discovered that "cancer" brings out my rational side.

When my thyroid enlarged to the point I could see it in the mirror, it wasn't the "whys" that plagued me, but the "how's." *If this is cancer, how will I cope with treatment? I'm a baby about needles and I have a phobia of hospitals. If this is cancer, how will I deal with my hair falling out? If this is cancer, how will I work and pay my bills? If this is cancer, how will I be able to serve at church like I want to, or will I be too sick?*

I didn't share these fears because they seemed so little in relation to the bigger picture, but since I already knew God would heal me one way or another, my rational mind could only see the practical concerns. I forbid myself to consider the life-changing ones. I told my mom and one friend and got really, brutally honest with God. I left it there, asked God to provide the money for the next round of tests and shut the door on it.

Then, God put on my heart to go to a worship night at my church. It was my first time there, but I felt like it was the right week to go. I was there to thank him for all he had done; for his faithfulness and goodness in spite of all the challenges. Near the end of the service, the pastor gave a word of knowledge that sent a warm feeling through my heart. He said that cancer was gone, that perfect love casts out all fear, and that "you are healed." The moment he said that, I felt the Holy Spirit fall around my shoulders and couldn't stop grinning. I claimed that word and felt perfect peace replace the fear that I had been fighting for the past month.

When I got home, there was no swelling around my thyroid. No nodules. No nothing. When I woke up, my neck was the smallest it had been in months. The mass was gone. I asked my mom, a nurse, if she noticed anything about my neck and she noticed instantly that the enlargement was gone.

I was healed.
I am healed.

I have no doubt. There is not a single cancercus cell in my thyroid. Not a single one.

What better way to end the year than to experience the manifestation of God's promise?

While this year has been brutal in so many ways, giving bruises and causing the occasional internal bleeding along the way, God has used every single piece for my good. The battles of this year tested and challenged me, the blessings reminded me that God was with me and was caring for me along the way, and the bruises are my proof that I came out on the other side and that no weapon formed against me prospered.

Satan's attempt to knock me out may have worked in the physical. I wasn't as social as I normally am, wasn't able to serve like I would've liked, to travel like I hoped or anything like that. From the outside, it was a really sucky year. But his attacks only backfired in the spiritual realm. In truth, this year was epic. What God did in me was epic. The change I see in myself is epic. The love that I now receive from my Father is beyond epic.

God gave me the analogy of a bulb planted at the end of fall. It sits, relatively dormant, in cold darkness all winter long sending roots deeper into the soil, away from the light. It makes for a lonely, cold winter, but those roots need darkness to grow, to expand, to strengthen because once spring comes and that plant shoots up out of the soil, those strong roots keep it in place and blooming through everything that comes against it.

From that perspective, I look back on my epic highlight reel and happily thank God for all he did and leave it behind me as I walk forward, believing for a year of blooming. A year of fruitfulness, of reaping the seeds sown in darkness, of enjoying my healing and restoration, of using my gifts, making new friends, meeting my husband - saying I'm not opposed, God-, and anything else God has planned for this year.

Come and listen, all you who fear God, and I will tell you what he did for me. Psalm 66:16

Inside a Russian Orphanage

Stephanie Reno

When you care about someone, your heart wants to express it. When you love people, you want to tell them.

I flew from Oklahoma to Russia to show the love of Jesus to children in orphanages. I traveled to Moscow knowing communication would be a major challenge. I didn't know their language and they didn't know mine. I felt unprepared, but I had to follow where God was leading me.

On one Saturday morning during my trip, I drove outside of Moscow to an orphanage for special needs children. I rode with a group of local Russians who regularly visited this orphanage. Therefore, they immediately dispersed to their different areas once we arrived and I was left to myself.

I stepped through the door into the girl's classroom section and was soon surrounded by preteen girls. Most of them stopped a foot away and looked at me, studying my face. They were accustomed to their regular visitors, but I could see their curiosity in a new visitor. I smiled at them and looked from face to face. Still stuck in the doorway of the classroom with a dozen eyes scanning me, uneasiness swept over me as I realized that they expected me to begin talking to them. Stumbling to introduce myself in Russian, I felt paralyzed and looked around for some kind of rescue. All I could do was smile and hope that they could sense that I wanted to be their friend.

I focused in on a sweet, cross-eyed girl standing next to me. I hunched down to be more on her level and put my hand on her shoulder. She said something in Russian that was too quiet for me to hear and then she wrapped her arms around me in a hug. Once the other girls saw that I was giving hugs, they all wanted one! At one time, I had three or four girls hugging me at once. They began talking very excitedly to me. I didn't know exactly what they were saying, but I smiled and laughed along with them.

A slim girl with big glasses, who looked about ten years old, clung to me as I tried to converse with one of the classroom teachers. The little girl's name was Nina and the teacher told me she had been in a foster home for a while, but had recently been returned to the orphanage. I hugged Nina for as long as she wanted and she eventually went off to play with some friends.

I left the orphanage a few hours later knowing I would probably never see those girls again. I wanted to tell them how they are loved. How they are not rejected. How someone from across the world came to tell them that I care about them and think about them and pray for them.

Later a woman was able to translate for me, but I wanted to look in their eyes and hold their hands and tell them how amazing they are to God. I wasn't able to do that. Even though my heart wasn't able to fully express my compassion and love for the girls there, I demonstrated my love in the best way I knew how. And I believe when we put our whole heart into something, the power of God can sweep far beyond our human ability. I was sincere in my love for them and that's all God needed to move through me.

Empowered to Win

Naomi Damron

It is with thanksgiving and praise to the Lord that I share with you my story.

There had been a history of successful Bible studies, written by several well-known authors on various topics which had blessed, encouraged and matured many women in our church. Our assignment in early January was to select the study of the Lord's choosing for that particular season.

We had prayed, searching in local Christian book stores and on the internet, yet did not have a clear direction. During a brief conversation on the phone with one of the other leaders and with no new possibilities to consider, we prayed again asking our Father to guide us by His Spirit into His perfect will. The start date of the Bible study was fast approaching; we were down to the wire.

Immediately after the phone was back on the hook, I had what I call "A Ten Minute Adventure with Jesus." In those minutes He gave me the title of the Bible study, the titles for eight sessions plus the titles of the five studies for each session. I quickly grabbed a pen and paper and began writing. I was astounded! I sat down and stared at what I had written, hardly believing my own eyes. Is this really happening to me? Is this the reason we had been unable to make a decision?

After spending some time praising and thanking the Lord for what I believed to be His direction, I called my friend again for her counsel, relating to her what had happened. She was thrilled and believed also this was God's direction for our group, being in total agreement. This was the course we should take. She also agreed to be my prayer partner during the process. Please know, before that day, writing a Bible study had never even crossed my mind. However, on that day in early January it seemed as if the Lord was saying, "I've given you the outline, now you fill in the blanks."

>All glory and praise to Him Who sits on the throne!!
>From His tool-box, with all my heart

That Still Small Voice

Doc Woods

I was coming home on Sunday evening from the construction site where I was building a log cabin for a family. It was being built not far from Willow Alaska. The cabin was sitting on a bluff above a gorgeous lake surrounded by white barked Birch trees. It was beautiful!

The drive took about an hour in order to return home to Anchorage.

About half way home I saw an old white Chrysler boiling down a dirt road headed directly for the paved highway I was traveling on (the Anchorage-Fairbanks highway). For some reason that vision has stuck in my mind. Something in my mind directed me to fully notice the car. A teenage girl was driving it, and the car was definitely traveling faster than was safe under the circumstances.

About a mile farther I came to the intersection of the Alaska Railroad and the highway.

The cross arms of the railroad crossing were down indicating that a train would be along soon.

As I pulled up behind the car ahead of me, that 'Still, Small Voice' urged me to pull up closer to the vehicle ahead. I have always left about five to ten feet between me and the vehicle ahead-whenever traffic stops in front of me. Never before or since have I felt so strongly that I should do such a thing. But, as directed by the voice I continued to creep closer and closer to the van that was stopped ahead of me.

The little voice kept urging me to move farther forward until I was literally about an inch from the van's rear bumper! Being that close to the car ahead of me, I put the car in park so that I would not inadvertently bump the car ahead of me.

Suddenly far behind me, I heard BAM! BAM! BAM! BAM! BAM! BAM! BAM! BAM! BAM! The sounds of destruction came nearer to me and nearer to me, each BAM sounding closer.

After the sounds of wreckage finally stopped, I got out of my car and discovered that the last car that had NOT been involved in the ten-car accident was mine! The front bumper of the car behind me came to rest an inch behind my rear bumper!

Had I not pulled forward as far as I did, I would have been involved in that accident.

The car that had caused the wreckage was the same white Chrysler I had noticed a mile or so back.

The Gift

Rosie Maureen

My relationship with my Mother was always complicated. She was addicted to one thing or another from the time she immigrated from her birth-land of Jamaica to arrive in the United States at the age of fourteen. She married my Dad at eighteen and gave birth to me at the age of twenty. He was a quiet man, steady and hard-working, openly loving the Lord and attending Mass three times a day no matter where his truck driving jobs took him. My Mother reflected on those years as the only time she was happy. Those were also the only times she can remember being drug free. He insisted that she go to church with him every day and she began to like it. She soon renounced Obeah, the Jamaican version of 'voodoo' to get to know her husband's so called 'white man's God ". She sewed me a Baptism dress, agreed to let me have Christian God-parents to guide me, and stood by his side for my Baptism.

At thirty-two, with no prior warnings, my father had a sudden and fatal heart attack. My mother blamed God for taking him away and all of her addictions returned which made my once safe life become a nightmare, constantly spiraling out of control. I was five when her endless grief became the new norm. My father's pictures were removed because she referred to his death as him "leaving" us. I was spanked if I mentioned his name and although I still used his last name my mother went back to her maiden name, retaining it, even after five additional and short lived marriages.

On Father's Day, his birthday, and their Valentine wedding anniversary, I would sneak out the pictures that she kept hidden in a box in the closet. I would see him smiling with me sitting in his lap and a modestly dressed, fresh faced Mother I could barely remember, beaming at us both. I would whisper his name like it was a guilty pleasure and scurry out before I was caught. Church was a taboo subject and when she found out I had attended a Vacation Bible camp with one of the neighbor's kids, she broke my collarbone which resulted in the first of many times she was jailed. I, at the age of ten, began my first rotation in the states foster care system.

Sooner or later, she would get an early release or be admitted into a new rehab program, in part because she was beautiful and charming. She vowed to do better, would accept the government's work programs, attend the meetings for her addictions and then in a matter of weeks after being released from incarcerated, she would slip up and have just one drink and begin the process over again.

From a practical point I was grateful for life. I was born a few years shy of Roe v. Wade and my Mother would remind me that I was lucky she had me as she had eliminated my unborn siblings. Still, she had given birth to me in spite of detesting pregnancy and children in general, because of the insistence of my father. So even though he was absent from Earth he was always present in my mind, simply because without him I would not have made it from her womb.

Years went on and my mother went from simply drinking, chain-smoking cigarettes and consuming large amounts of marijuana to dabbling in meth, cocaine and finally crack. By the time she got hooked on heroin she didn't have the energy to love herself let alone anyone else. I finished high school at seventeen and moved as far away from her as I could. I married and had a daughter of my own, but did not give my mother my new address or let her know my married name. I worked an extra part time job and sent that entire check to her each week to make sure she had something.

Free from her hatred of God, I was able to look into the faith that my father had which let him find joy in a childhood besought by the segregation of Mississippi and the early death of his own mother. When my mother finally overdosed alone, shortly after her 40th birthday, I felt grief but also a sense of relief that waiting for her to die was over. I took no comfort in the fact that she boldly hated God to the last moment but tried to find comfort in the fact that my father loved the Lord and one day we would meet in Heaven.

As the years went by, I maintained a close relationship with God but there was a still a barrier.

I would read the Gospels about the Father God being so loving and wonder how could he like me; love me maybe, but could he like me? After all, none of my stepfathers had. I wondered if my biological father had lived, would he have cared or would he have divorced my Mother after a while like my stepfathers did? Would I have been dismissed as an annoyance or would he have tossed me up in the air or hugged me at the end of the day? I wished that my Mother was alive just so I could have someone around who had known him. All of the photos from my childhood were gone but I would close my eyes and go back into the closet of my past and remember his shy grin. He must have loved me a little, right? I knew that these doubts were from Satan but soon I was having nightmares about running to my dad and having him turn away.

I began the New Year reading a Bible study that takes you through the entire Bible in 365 days. By reading a bit a day and then going over it, I found areas I had overlooked. One day I came across (King James Bible) *"If ye then, being evil, know how to give good gifts unto your children, how much more shall your Father which is in heaven give good things to them that ask him?"*-Matthew 7:11 and then Luke 11:13 *If you then, though you are evil, know how to give good gifts to your children, how much more will your Father in heaven give the Holy Spirit to those who ask him!"* and also :"James 1:17 *"Every good and perfect gift is from above, coming down from the Father of the heavenly lights, who does not change like shifting shadows."*

It was near my birthday and I wondered what it would be like if my dad had given me a birthday gift. He died when I was a few months' shy of five and although I had a few family pictures there were none of birthday parties. My mother never liked that kind of fuss, and I don't remember any treasured doll or mention of any trinket that he may have left behind.

I prayed 'Lord, I know that I do not need to ask for signs but it would be a wonderful birthday present if I could have the peace of knowing that my father loved me. I know it says do not call anyone on earth 'father,' for you have one Father, and he is in heaven, but sometimes I am unsure.

The day of my birthday came and I was sent many well wishes. A friend of mine emailed me a government site link. She said she had clicked on it not expecting anything but had found that she had unclaimed money from a real estate transaction years ago. Since my husband, who was an 18-wheeler big rig truck driver, and I had moved over a dozen times maybe we had "lost" money too. I clicked it in my husband's name and found that he had a windfall of $5.95 cents left in a long forgotten account.

Then I did my own in my married and maiden name. An insurance policy came up. My father, who had so little, had taken out a life insurance policy for me.

My Father was a day worker and he was trying to support my mother's often overwhelming spending habits as well as save for a small house, but through it all he was thinking ahead about how to love me.

Through all the hard years with her overwhelming poverty, my mother never touched the insurance account (or perhaps she didn't know), but I believe it was left for me to find it when I needed it the most.

Not financially, but spiritually as a reminder.

I _was_ loved. I was always loved by my earthy father and by the Father God of today and yesterday and tomorrow.

I did not claim my "lost" money; I left it for the grandchildren I hope to have one day. Every once in a while, I click on the link and remind myself my father gave me the greatest gift he ever could by openly loving God in spite of all the obstacles he faced. His faith leads me home and that is the greatest gift of all.

Eighteen Days After Her Death

Michelle Lehman

My mom died May 9th, 2011.

Biologically, she was my grandmother, but she raised me, and therefore, she *is* my mother. Not a day goes by that I don't miss her something fierce, and even as I write these words, it's difficult to see through my tear-filled eyes.

She was Pentecostal – long hair tied up in buns, long-sleeved blouses tucked into those long skirts. She worked hard in the home to raise me, and did so with a truly unconditional love. Every meal was hot, every bath time was bubbly, and she sat in bed next to me every night telling me stories and singing me songs until I fell asleep. Sheets turned into forts that she happily crawled through on her hands and knees in that long skirt.

She let me paint pictures with my watercolors, seated at her coffee table without so much as a towel down, when other parents would never have let a little one do such a thing for fear of a mess. She taught me how to shave my legs, even though she didn't want me wearing shorts. She took me to buy my prom dresses even though she didn't approve of the amount of skin they would show.

I was an easy child that turned into a not-so-easy teenager. I made straight A's, didn't drink, didn't run around, didn't do any of the things most parents would consider "difficult" to raise, but I wasn't Pentecostal. I didn't go to church, and I thought God was the most ridiculous idea that anyone had ever dreamed up.

Sometimes, we fought; the magnitude of those fights is still something that haunts me. The yelling I did, the tears she cried, the truly hurtful words I screamed out in anger over being 16 years old, being pushed to find God and follow a 'false' prophet such as Jesus.

It was preposterous! It was horrible not to be trusted on my own as a human being. I told her more than once, "I don't need your God when I am otherwise good on my own!"

Eventually, I grew up and moved away; I got my first real job and bought a home. She was always so proud of my house and my life. When I got my first new car as an adult and drove it "home" to see her, the joy on her face was immeasurable.

We had always been so poor. I didn't realize it growing up because I had everything I ever wanted, but we were. I'm sure there were times she worried about paying the bills while still buying me those prom dresses, but she made sure to do both.

Throughout my adult years, she would mention God in her subtle ways; she knew how I felt about it, so she didn't dare lecture me. When we talked on the phone, she would tell me a story about a blessing she had received and finish her sentence with "Praise the Lord for that." When I'd return home for the holidays or monthly visits, we'd never be allowed to eat until she said the blessing over the meal. I still rolled my eyes to the back of my head even as a "mature" adult because it was so ridiculous to me and I couldn't for the life of me understand why an otherwise intelligent woman would be so childish as to believe in something of which she had no proof.

In March of 2011, I was sitting on my couch watching a movie. It wasn't a particularly important movie, probably some type of romantic comedy (those are still my favorite), but as I sat there watching, something drastic happened to me. All of a sudden, without warning, my body physically jolted up and off that couch, grabbing my chest because I couldn't breathe; the wind had been knocked out of me entirely and I BELIEVED THERE WAS A GOD!

God was tired of waiting on me to figure it out on my own, so he literally knocked some sense into me.

I immediately called my dearest friend to ask her if I could join her for church that Sunday. I went, and it was as if I had been transported to another world. I could feel the power inside of me and that was all the proof I needed. I didn't tell my grandmother right away because I was embarrassed that I had been wrong all those years, and I didn't want to deal with having to admit it.

But over the next few weeks, God moved in me.

He told me, "You need to go see her every weekend instead of once a month. You need to call her more often, you need to make some memories you've been putting off."

So I did.

We went for car rides seeing the countryside. We went for pizza (our favorite thing). We had a garage sale at her house where she enjoyed the conversation with the people who stopped to browse.

By this time in her life, she was quite frail. Truth be told, she had never been in very good health even when I was growing up, but now, she was truly aged and had such pain in her eyes with every step she hobbled.

We planned a garage sale, I stayed the night at her house for the first time since moving away. When she tucked me into bed that night as a 29-year-old woman, I kissed her sweet hand, and to this day, I can still feel my lips on her skin.

What a blessing she was in my life!

By this point, it was the last weekend in April, and we laughed, talked, and enjoyed ourselves at the sale. I don't think we sold more than $20.00 worth of knick-knacks all day, but that wasn't why we did it.

I didn't realize it at the time, but God was preparing me. He knew I wouldn't live a day past her death if I didn't have peace in my own heart or those extra precious memories at the end.

A few days after the sale, I called her, but she couldn't come to the phone; my grandpa said she wasn't feeling well and had laid down to nap. She laid in that bed for three days before they called for an ambulance. I met them at the hospital and stayed for the next three days. She wasn't lucid, but I know she knew I was there.

I held her hand. I talked to her. I sang songs – the same songs she sang to me when I was little. God had prepared me for this exact time!

As she lay in that hospital bed, I told her it was okay for her to go because I knew what she had meant all those years, and that I believed! I told her it was okay for her to go because as much as I loved her, she didn't need to stick around for me. My heart was right, and she could go knowing that I finally got it and I wouldn't give up.

Her blood pressure was so low that the machines were beeping loudly; her body was shutting down. Her little toes started kicking in that bed, and I know at that point, she was running straight to Jesus.

I was holding her hand when her heart stopped, the same hand that I had kissed only a week before.

Eighteen days after her death, on May 29th, 2011, I accepted Jesus Christ into my heart in the same church I had started attending only months before. I could barely get through the prayer because I was bawling so hard that I couldn't see the pastor's wife standing there with me trying to get me through it.

But when I finished praying, I felt God inside me saying, "It's okay, your grandma sees you and she knows."

He prepared me for her death as he prepared me for eternal life. I'm confident that when I die at the end of my time, she'll be there waiting.

Go in the Power of God!

CPSIA information can be obtained
at www.ICGtesting.com
Printed in the USA
FSOW02n1727310316
18611FS

9 780986 233159